Raph's Tale

Raph's Tale

By Dan Shapiro, MD

Illustrations by John Watkins-Chow

Published by Dagmar Miura
Los Angeles
www.dagmarmiura.com

Raph's Tale

Copyright © 2020 Dan Shapiro, MD
All rights reserved. No part of this book may be used or reproduced in any manner whatsoever without prior written permission except in the case of brief quotations embodied in critical articles or reviews. For information, address the author at drdan@parentchildjourney.com.

This is a work of fiction. Names, characters, businesses, places, events, and incidents are either the products of the author's imagination or used in a fictitious manner. Any resemblance to actual persons, living or dead, or actual events is purely coincidental.

First published 2020

ISBN: 978-1-951130-37-4

*With love,
For Ella and Charlie,
Two birds of a different feather
(DS)*

*For Dawn, who makes me want to be a better person,
and Kara & Lea, who let me know why that's important
(JWC)*

Contents

Raph's Tale	1
History of *Raphus cucullatus*	54
History of the Tambalacoque Tree	58
Neurodiversity Lives	61
Raph's Tale Coloring Book	63
About the Author	66
About the Illustrator	67

Hawk soared high over the river. Down below, he saw a little boat with a funny-looking bird. It was drifting downstream, toward Great Falls. Hawk flew down and perched on the boat. Hawk screeched, "You're going to kill yourself staying in that tiny tub! Fly away, you stupid bird!"

But the strange bird just stood there in its boat and said, "I would if I could."

Hawk couldn't believe it: "What kind of bird doesn't even know how to fly?"

The odd bird answered, "Raphus cucullatus, of course. You can call me Raph." Then Raph added, "I want Tambalacoque."

Well, Hawk had never heard of a Raphus cucullatus bird—or Tambalacoque. All Hawk knew was that Raph was soon to be a goner. Great Falls was roaring louder and louder. Hawk grabbed Raph in his talons and flapped his wings—hard. Hawk didn't get twenty feet before realizing that Raph was just too heavy. So Hawk dropped Raph back on the boat and thought, "Not much more I can do here."

Hawk started to fly away, but Raph called out, "I want Tambalacoque."

Hawk muttered, "What am I getting myself into?" Hawk sighed, swooped back down, and perched on the back of the boat. Hawk's talons dug deep into the stern. Hawk's wings flapped hard. The little boat moved up the river, far away from the falls. Raph was safe, but Hawk was exhausted. No way could Hawk push Raph's boat all the way up the river. What to do?

Just then, for no good reason, Raph said, "I want to go back down the river."

Hawk said, "Remember Great Falls. Raph, you need to go up the river!"

Raph said, "No, I don't. I don't care about Great Falls!"

Hawk yelled, "You have to do as I say!"

Again, Raph yelled back, "No, I don't!"

Back and forth they fought. The little boat rocked from side to side. Before they knew it, they'd thrown each other overboard. Underwater, they struggled to breathe—but they kept on fighting.

Finally, the fight ended. Maybe Hawk won the fight. Or maybe Hawk just gave up. Who can remember? And what did it matter? Raph and Hawk drifted backward in the cold water. The boat drifted beside them. The sound of Great Falls was getting even louder. Somehow, Hawk and Raph dragged themselves back onto the boat. Hawk flapped and pushed the boat ashore, safe once more. Staying at different ends of the boat, not saying a word, they caught their breath. Just then, a round fruit fell out of a tree and into the boat.

Raph cried, "Tambalacoque!" and ate it with one joyful gulp.

Hawk smiled and said to himself, "So that's what Tambalacoque is." At that moment, Hawk knew they were in this boat together.

As they fell asleep, exhausted, Hawk wondered, What kind of bird is this anyhow?

In the morning, Hawk and Raph started up the river. The current was strong. It wasn't long before they ran into trouble. There were logs. There was lightning. There were rocks. It wasn't easy traveling.

After a while, Hawk decided that they should take a break and just let the boat drift ashore. They pulled up on the bank. Raph was relieved to get back on land. Hawk was glad to perch up in a tree. First Raph pooped. Then Raph kicked a pebble into the water and watched it skip across the surface. Raph glanced up to see if Hawk was watching. Hawk smiled. Raph kicked another pebble. It skipped even farther. Raph looked up again. Hawk flew down and tried kicking a pebble like Raph did. They had fun kicking pebbles together.

Raph said, "I didn't know hawks kicked pebbles."

Hawk said, "I didn't know hawks kicked pebbles either."

They both laughed. Then Hawk flew off high into the sky. Hawk had been stuck on the boat with Raph awhile. It felt good to be airborne again. After a good fly, Hawk collected a few more Tambalacoque fruit and came back to Raph.

Hawk squawked at Raph, "Time to get back on the boat."

But Raph didn't seem to hear. Raph was too busy kicking pebbles. Hawk squawked again. Nothing. So Hawk tickled Raph's tail tuft.

Raph looked up: "What?"

Hawk squawked to come. Hawk pointed to the boat. Raph looked confused. Finally, Hawk just got on the boat.

"Oh," cooed Raph. "Why didn't you say so?"

But Raph was never eager to leave the shore and get back on the boat. Raph always wanted to kick "just one more" pebble. Hawk tried different ways to get Raph back onboard. Sometimes Raph came if Hawk sang and danced in the air.

Sometimes Hawk squawked and sang, but Raph still wouldn't stop playing on the shore.

So Hawk just flew to the boat and waited. Raph kept on playing. But suddenly, Raph looked up and thought, Where's Hawk? For a moment, Raph was scared. Raph ran fast back to the boat. There was Hawk, patiently perched.

Sometimes Raph just wouldn't get back on the boat at all—unless, of course, Hawk promised Raph a Tambalacoque fruit.

And then there were times when nothing seemed to work. Hawk wanted to get going, but Raph could be a stubborn bird.

Hawk would say, "Let's go."

Raph would say, "I want to stay on shore and kick more pebbles."

So they talked and worked out a compromise; like, five more pebble kicks, and then Raph gets to help steer. OK? OK. And so they'd go, back up the river. Together.

Hawk had never been a navigator, but the more they traveled, the better he became.

RAPH'S TALE

If there were logs, they could just cruise the boat right over the tops of them.

If there was lightning, Hawk carried
Raph off the river and onto a safe island.

And if there was a rock, Hawk could stop the boat. Floating, still, in front of the rock, they would pause to consider their reflections in the water. Hawk saw Hawk. Raph saw Raph. And then, Hawk and Raph saw themselves looking at each other.

Mile by mile, in sputters and spurts, they continued their journey. Hawk taught Raph how to handle the boat. On bad days, they hit some rocks and the boat leaked. They used Tambalacoque shells to bail the water. They used poop to patch the holes. Raph hated bailing and patching. Hawk did too, but they had no choice.

On good days, when there was a strong wind at their backs, they hoisted sail and spread their wings. Hawk's wings were so big. Raph's wings were so little.

Raph knew, I can't fly like other birds. But when they caught the wind just right, Raph felt like their boat could fly!

One day, Hawk flew away and never came back. Raph let go of the wheel and sat down in the boat. Alone. Raph let the boat drift all the way back down the river. Raph watched the shoreline pass by. After a while, Raph noticed that everywhere they'd stopped, little Tambalacoque trees were beginning to grow. The fruit they'd eaten. The seeds they'd pooped. The pebbles they'd kicked to drive those seeds into the ground. The farther Raph drifted downriver, the taller the trees. Each Tambalacoque tree was stronger and more majestic than the last. Then there were a few with little buds. And finally, Raph saw a few Tambalacoque trees bearing large, ripe fruit.

Raph called out, "I want Tambalacoque!" Magically, one Tambalacoque fruit appeared in the water, bobbing and floating right up to the boat. Raph caught the sweet fruit in its beak. Raph took a bite—and smiled. Then, he fell asleep.

Raph woke up on shore. He looked around and wondered, How did I get here? Hawk was gone. Their boat was gone. He did not see even one Tambalacoque fruit tree. Raph wondered, "Where am I? What can I eat?" Raph's wings were too small for flying. But his legs were strong and sturdy. So Raph started to walk. And walk. And walk. After a long time, Raph's legs got tired, and his tummy got hungry. What to do?

Just then, a dog appeared. Running circles around Raph, the dog barked, "Ruff!" Raph said, "My name is not Ruff. It's Raph." The dog repeated, "Ruff!"

Again, Raph said, "My name is Raph!" Even though the dog couldn't say Raph's name right, at least Raph wasn't alone anymore. The dog was happy to meet Raph too, and jumped and ran and barked. The dog came close to Raph, barked, then ran away again.

Raph said, "I'd like to play chase but I'm too tired." Then Raph said, "That's what I'll call you: Chase. Chase the Dog."

The dog growled. "Okay, then," said Raph, "I'll just call you Dog." Dog wagged his tail in agreement.

Raph saw a smooth bump on a log. A perfect place to sit and rest.

Raph settled his tuft down onto the bump. "Ahh," sighed Raph. "What a nice bump for sitting."

With a muffled voice, the bump protested, "Get off of me, you strange bird! I'm not a bump on a log. That's my shell. I'm a turtle, warming myself in the sun. You are too heavy and you're blocking my ultraviolet light!" Startled that the bump could talk, Raph climbed off and said, "I'm sorry, Bump. I didn't know you were a turtle."

The turtle said, "Please don't call me Bump. Call me Turtle!"

Raph said, "Okay, Turtle."

Raph was getting hungrier. But he was too tired to walk another step. Raph asked Dog and Turtle, "Can you get me some Tambalacoque fruit?" Dog barked. Raph looked up the trail. Turtle said, "I've heard that there is a whole forest of Tambalacoque trees over the mountain." At the end of the trail, far, far away, there loomed a very large mountain. "Up over that mountain?" Raph asked. "How would we get there? How could we get to the other side?"

Excited for an adventure, Dog ran every which way, barking "Ruff!" Raph agreed with Dog: "Yes, you're right. It would be a very rough trip. But you sure seem excited to go anyhow."

Turtle was petrified at the thought of leaving his log. Turtle whimpered, "Oh, no," and hid deep within his shell.

Just then, Raph saw something on the ground: a unicycle. Raph thought aloud, "That's how I can get to the mountain. I can't fly, and it's too far to walk. But with my strong legs and my hind tuft, a unicycle would be perfect."

Dog barked encouragement. Turtle groaned, "You've got to be crazy. Birds don't ride unicycles!" But Raph's tuft settled softly onto the unicycle seat. His feet fit on the pedals.

Dog ran ahead, yapping and woofing. Turtle stayed on his log, screaming at Raph and Dog, "Stop, you fools! You won't make it to the mountain. You'll fall off that one-wheeled contraption. Don't leave me here alone!" But Raph and Dog were too excited. Raph tightened his leg muscles.

He sang, "To the mountain we go!" He leaned forward. The wheel turned—but only once. The unicycle hit a rock, and Raph went airborne.

For a moment, he marveled, "Maybe I can fly after all?" But Raph came right down—hard. With a buried beak but a racing heart, Raph thought, Rough landing. Dog agreed: "Ruff!" Turtle said, "You must be completely dodo! You could have gotten yourself killed!"

Raph's beak began to hurt. He started to wonder, Maybe Turtle was right. Maybe birds can't ride unicycles. Turtle said, "I told you so. Just stay on this log with me. That way, you won't get hurt. You can rest. If you fall asleep, you can dream about Tambalacoque fruit."

Raph thought, If I get on the unicycle and try to chase Dog, I go too fast and fall on my beak. If I try walking or just sit like Turtle, I go too slow and never find any Tambalacoque fruit.

Then Raph had an idea: I could ride the unicycle a little like Dog and a little like Turtle. If I lean forward—just a little—I could go forward but not fall on my beak. If I lean back—just a little—I could slow down but not fall on my tuft.

Raph tried to find the right balance. Sometimes he got too excited and fell forward. Sometimes he got too scared and fell backward. But, instead of hurting his beak or his tuft, Raph learned to land on his feet. At first, he could make it just one roll of the wheel. Then two. Then, very gradually, Raph learned how to lean and pedal just right. Seven rolls! Then twelve!

Dog kept running too far ahead. Turtle lagged farther behind. But Raph made progress down the trail. Excited but cautious, moving ahead but not too fast, Raph got better at keeping his balance. He rode for longer distances without falling at all. The mountain grew closer and closer.

Dog ran ahead and got to the mountain first. Raph rode his unicycle and got there second. Finally, even Turtle crawled his way there. They were all thrilled to have finished the trail. But after such a long journey, there were still no Tambalacoque trees. How to get over the mountain? It was too steep and too high. Raph's hungry tummy rumbled.

At first, Raph felt sad. Then, Raph's sadness became anger, and, much to his surprise, his anger turned into rage! They had come so far. Now this! Raph exploded, screaming furiously at Dog and Turtle and anybody else who could hear: "Who put this mountain here anyhow? I need my Tambalacoque!" With each anguished screech, Raph smashed his beak into the mountain. Again and again, he cried out and chiseled away.

Turtle pleaded, "What are you doing? You're going to break your beak!"

Raph shrieked at Turtle, "If we can't get over this mountain, we'll have to dig right through it!"

Dog agreed, "Ruff!" and started pawing away at the mountain. Turtle thought for a second, then put out his forelegs and started burrowing away at the mountain too.

Raph thought, I didn't know turtles could dig. The three friends dug together.

Then came the most surprising thing of all. Suddenly, Raph, Dog, and Turtle were not alone. Many other animals had been hiding at the base of the mountain. They wanted to help. Some had gotten to the other side themselves, but knew many of their friends weren't able to. Some had tried but failed. Many had never even thought about trying. But Raph's angry screeching had brought them all out.

The sight of a bird, a dog, and a turtle all digging at the mountain together inspired the other animals. Maybe there was a way to the other side for everyone after all.

One by one, then by the dozens, and then by the hundreds, animals came, of every size and shape, to help dig a tunnel. Together, side by side, stone by stone, they punched their way through the center of the mountain. With so many animals digging, it didn't take long. Joyfully, they pushed Raph to the front, insisting that he be the first one through the opening. And there, just as Raph remembered: Tambalacoque trees. Tall and loaded with fruit. Plenty for everybody. Tambalacoque fruit had never tasted so good.

History of Raphus cucullatus

In the Indian Ocean, off the southeast coast of Africa, is a huge island called Madagascar. Just a bit farther east is a tiny island called Mauritius. There, in the woods near the water, lived a bird named *Raphus cucullatus;* or for short, as affectionately nicknamed in this book, Raph. This bird was descended from a proud old family of pigeons and doves. But in many ways, Raph was a bird of a different feather.

Raph was a big bird, standing more than three feet tall and weighing more than thirty pounds. Raph had brown-gray feathers all over its body, a little extra tuft of feathers for a tail, but no feathers at all on its head. In fact, Raph's last name, cucullatus, means "wearing a hood." Raph's beak was very large: black, yellow, and red, with a huge bulb for smelling. Like a turkey, Raph kept rocks in its gizzard for grinding up swallowed food. Raph's wings were too weak to fly. But with big yellow feet and strong sturdy legs, Raph could walk around just fine. And there was plenty of ground food, mostly nuts and fruits.

Raph's favorite fruit was the Tambalacoque, a round, juicy kind of peach with a woody pit containing its seeds. Raph enjoyed picking up Tambalacoque fruit with its beak and grinding up the pit with stones in its gizzard.

On the little island of Mauritius, Raph had plenty of friends and no enemies. With nothing to fear, there was no need to fly. Raph only needed to lay one egg at a time to ensure its family's survival.

Even if Raph was a different kind of bird, Mauritius suited Raph just fine. And in one very special way, Raph suited the island of Mauritius.

Not only did Raph get big eating Tambalacoque fruit, the Tambalacoque tree flourished thanks to Raph. Each time Raph ate Tambalacoque fruit, seeds germinated in Raph's intestines.

With each poop, Raph disseminated Tambalacoque seeds. The more Tambalacoque fruit Raph ate, the more Tambalacoque seeds were planted. A win-win, bird-tree relationship! Talk about recycling! Propagation through defecation!

For thousands of years, there were no human beings on the island of Mauritius. But then, starting in the 1500s, Portuguese explorers made occasional visits. The Raphinae family's first sustained encounters with people were not until about 1600, when Dutch sailors came to Mauritius. They had never seen birds like Raph. These birds didn't know flight or fear. They were defenseless and naive. The Dutch easily killed them, ate them, and destroyed their habitat. The Dutch boats also brought cats, rats, pigs, and monkeys. These nonnative animals ate the Raphinae family's eggs. Extinction came quickly.

This strange bird is now known as the "dodo." It's not clear how such a derogatory name originated. The most generous explanation is that "dodo" might have been an approximation of the bird's call, a two-note pigeon-like sound, "doo-doo." More likely, and still not so bad, "dodo" might have been a term related to the Dutch word Dodaars, which means either "fat-arse" or "knot-arse," referring to the tuft of feathers on its hind end. But because these flightless and fearless birds were so easily caught, it's likely that "dodo" came from the Dutch word *dodoor* for "sluggard" or the Portuguese word *doudo* (currently *doido*), meaning "fool" or "crazy." Despite this uncertainty about origins, everybody today knows to "go the way of the dodo" means to be "dead as a dodo" because you clearly must have been "stupid as a dodo."

The last living bird from the Raphinae family was seen in 1662. But the name "dodo"—and a very important message—lives on.

History of the Tambalacoque Tree

Sideroxylon grandiflorum, known as the Tambalacoque tree, is endemic to the island of Mauritius. It is a majestic tree with many strong roots and sprawling, thick branches that provide plenty of shade. Each tree normally lives for hundreds of years.

As you have already read, the Raphinae family needed the Tambalacoque tree for food, and the tree needed the bird to be its "Johnny Appleseed." Up through its extinction in the seventeenth century, Raphinae ate the Tambalacoque fruit and spread the seeds. Because of this mutually beneficial relationship, the Tambalacoque became known as the "dodo tree." But if so linked in life, what would keep the "dodo" and "dodo tree" from being likewise linked in death? Was the Tambalacoque tree too dependent on the Raphinae?

Over the centuries, since the last of the Raphinae died, there has been a steady decline in the number of Tambalacoque trees. But this sad story has a hopeful epilogue. Ironically, the rapid extinction of the Raphinae helped inspire the wildlife conservation movement. Raphus became a powerful early "poster bird" for protection of other endangered species. Locally, alarmed by the dodo bird's fate, Mauritians devoted themselves to saving its namesake tree. Globally, recognition of the bird and tree's mutual decline served as a cautionary tale about the interconnection of all life. To whatever degree Raph's extinction endangered the Tambalacoque, their relationship shed light on the importance of protecting individual species for the sake of entire ecosystems.

The seventeenth century was a terrible time to be a flightless bird. There were no conservationists around to save the Raphinae. But their extinction made the twenty-first century a more encouraging time for the Tambalacoque tree. Legions now rally to protect the Tambalacoque tree and the diversity of all natural life. One can only wonder: What if Raph was alive today? Would it be listed as an endangered species? Would hunting be illegal? Would people defend its habitat? Moreover, would it still be called a dodo bird?

Neurodiversity Lives

Decade by decade, more children are being identified with all types of developmental disabilities. Many complicated factors account for this rise. Much of the increase is because of broader diagnostic categories, better identification, and heightened sensitivity. Children with special needs have always been around. But they have been hidden from view in basements, institutions, and prisons, or otherwise marginalized by blame, shame, and derogatory names. Relatively "flightless" but completely innocent, they are not "dodos." They are our children. They are us. And we are all in the same boat together. With limited resources, our crisis—our challenge—is how to provide services, education, and jobs for the growing number of children and adults with special needs.

Despite this crisis—perhaps because of it—the twenty-first century has become a much more hopeful time to have a child with developmental differences. These children are finally getting recognition and help. The Americans with Disabilities Act prohibits discrimination against individuals with disabilities. The Individuals with Disabilities Education Act guarantees early intervention, special education, and related services to infants, children, and adolescents with disabilities. The disability rights and inclusion movements grow stronger every year. A powerful army of parents, providers, educators, and researchers have spearheaded a truly revolutionary change in sensitivity, expertise, and advocacy. Brain science and developmental practice continue to advance at an extraordinary pace. There is a growing awareness of the need to keep neurodiversity alive. We are only as great as our compassion for one another, not despite but because of our wonderful differences.

Raph's Tale Coloring Book

On the next few pages, color Raph your own way. Then go to parentchildjourney.com/raphcolors to color all the pictures in this book.

About the Author

Dr. Dan Shapiro is a native of East Lansing, Michigan. He moved to Washington, DC, to attend the George Washington University School of Medicine and stayed for pediatric residency training at Children's National Medical Center. Dr. Shapiro practiced primary-care pediatric and adolescent medicine in Silver Spring, Maryland, then shifted his focus to developmental and behavioral pediatrics. Currently, in addition to his office practice, Dr. Shapiro observes children and collaborates with educators at dozens of Washington, DC, and suburban Maryland schools. He developed ParentChildJourney.com, a comprehensive set of parent training and support programs. He is a fellow of the American Academy of Pediatrics and a member of the Society for Developmental and Behavioral Pediatrics. Dr. Shapiro is married, with four children and two grandchildren. He is the author of *Parent Child Journey: An Individualized Approach to Raising Your Challenging Child* and *Parent Child Excursions: ADHD, Anxiety and Autism*.

About the Illustrator

John Watkins-Chow was born in New Jersey and somehow ended up with three degrees from MIT, which he has failed to parlay into anything noteworthy. John has been drawing all of his life. He illustrated Dr. Shapiro's first two books. Otherwise, this book is likely the first place nongeek (and geek-adjacent) folk might see his art. He has been fortunate to work in animation, comics, and sketch card art on properties such as *Star Wars, Lord of the Rings,* and Marvel Comics—and very occasionally, his own comic, *Talismen*. During the day, John teaches math at a private school in suburban Maryland. When not producing sketchy art or stumbling in the classroom, John can reliably be found in the doghouse, a source of frustration for his lovely wife and embarrassment for his two talented daughters.

CPSIA information can be obtained
at www.ICGtesting.com
Printed in the USA
BVHW020204090920
588427BV00022B/724